The Elephant

Peaceful Giant

Text and Photos
by Christine and Michel Denis-Huot

Charlesbridge

Seen from an airplane, elephants seem small, but don't be fooled.
Full-grown elephants are more than 10 feet high.

In Africa

As the sun rises over the horizon, a new day dawns on the African plains. Lions roar in the distance, and the birds begin to sing.

The grass is green because the rainy season has already begun. Heavy, black clouds roll in. The elephants have spent the night sleeping under the acacia trees. Now the herd is ready to leave the trees. Silently, these huge animals march onto the plain.

Females lead the herd

The herd includes all the mothers and their babies. The oldest female is the leader and guides the herd. When she stops, everyone stops. When she starts again, all the other elephants follow her.

When the leader signals with a flap of her ears or a movement of her head, the herd gets ready to move.

The herd of elephants looks like a parade as it follows its leader across the plains.

Elephants tell each other how they feel by touching each other with their trunks, sniffing, and rubbing up against each other.

Elephants also talk to each other by making a wide range of sounds. Like whales, they can make some very low sounds that people can hear only with the help of special scientific instruments.

Herons eat insects kicked up by the elephants' footsteps.

To drink, the elephant sucks water into its trunk and squirts it into its mouth. An adult elephant needs about 20 gallons of water per day.

Elephants are very smart. During the dry season, when the riverbeds are empty, the elephants dig holes to find underground water.

Leaves, grasses, fruit, bark, and wood are food for the elephant.

What an appetite!

The herds stop to eat often. Elephants like to eat tender grasses as well as the branches of trees. They are big eaters. An adult can eat 300 pounds of food a day. To eat this much takes about 16 hours each day.

Elephants help spread the seeds of the fruits they eat, and are responsible for the growth of many new trees.

Elephants use their tusks and trunks to pull the tasty bark off the trees. Unfortunately, the trees often die from these injuries.

A giant nomad

Calmly and steadily, the herd travels far each day — 20 to 30 miles. In spite of their great weight, the elephants move silently through the underbrush.

Noontime. It is very hot! Antelopes take cover in the shade of the trees. The elephants fan their huge ears to cool themselves. Sometimes, using their trunks, they blow dust all over themselves to keep the insects away.

The trunk is really a terrific tool. It has so many muscles that it can move in all directions. The two edges or lips of the trunk are very sensitive and can pick up things as small as a peanut. The trunk can be used as a hand, a nose, a vacuum, or even a trumpet!

An elephant's skin is very thick and rough.

The trunk is wrinkled like an accordion. It is almost as long as the elephant is tall, so elephants must hold up their trunks when they walk.

10

Elephants walk on the tips of their toes, like horses do. The African elephant has four toenails on its front feet and three on its back feet.

When it is covered with dust, the elephant is the same color as the ground.

What big ears you have! They are about three feet wide. Even though the elephant is a mammal, it has very little hair or fur — except for the tuft at the end of its tail.

Males over twenty years old live alone, far from the families and other males.

The fighting males

Today, the males come to look for a mate. Three of them are interested in one female. The biggest one chases off the other two. After mating, the male does not stay long.

Twenty-two months later, a baby elephant will be born. It will weigh about 220 pounds and stand about 34 inches tall. After only an hour, it can stand up and follow the herd.

The baby drinks its mother's milk with its mouth. It has to roll up its little trunk to get it out of the way — not an easy thing to do!

Loving Mothers

Baby elephants drink their mother's milk until they are about two years old. When they are about four months old, they begin to eat some plants, too. All the females take care of the babies, patting and sniffing them tenderly.

When a baby cries, it sounds like a big, creaking door. The herd responds by stopping in its tracks. The mother rushes to her baby and places the tip of her trunk in the baby's mouth to calm it.

Baby elephants are born with red or black hairs on their heads, legs, and backs.

Elephants do not walk while holding each other's tails like they do in cartoons, but sometimes, babies make a game of grabbing the tail of a grown-up!

14

A fallen tree blocks the road the elephants are following. The baby elephant cannot step over it. What will the baby do? Its big sisters come to the rescue and move the tree.

The baby's trunk gets in the way. The trunk swings in all directions. The baby does not know what to do with it, and even steps on it now and then. All the little ones are very clumsy with those noses that are just too long! After awhile, each one will learn how to use it.

The baby is tired. Several times a day, it lies down next to its mother and rests.

The baby often extends its trunk to smell things. At birth, it has to recognize its mother by her smell, because it can hardly see anything at all.

The *real* king of the beasts

The elephants walk peacefully across the plains. Suddenly, they stop and point their trunks in the same direction. Lions are coming. Several big mothers form a circle around the babies. The others follow the leader of the herd as she charges toward the lions with a sound like the blaring of trumpets. The lions run away as fast as they can.

No animal would dare to attack an adult elephant who has such fierce tusks. The tusks are actually teeth that never stop growing. At birth, the baby has tiny tusks. At about two years old, the tusks have grown enough to begin to show. Elephants use their tusks to pull bark off trees, to dig holes, or to dig up roots.

Lions, hyenas, and crocodiles are the only enemies of the baby elephant.

When the baby elephants are in danger, the adults form a circle around them.

Worried about her baby, a mother charges toward an intruder. When face to face with an animal 10 feet high and weighing four and a half tons, the only thing to do is run!

Crossing rivers is not a problem even for the little ones. They are excellent swimmers.

It's easy to use a trunk like a shower. Just suck up some water and blow it out!

Mud protects the elephant's skin from the sun and from insects.

Water games

In the intense heat, the elephants are happy to come to a river. As they take a bath, they squirt water playfully and have a lot of fun. Before they leave, they roll in the mud along the riverbank.

Elephants can live in many places as long as they have enough water. Elephants can live in the forests, on the plains, on the mountainsides, and on the borders of deserts.

Young and old push and chase each other, climb on top of each other, and make great splashes in the water as they play.

The road to wisdom

The baby elephants are now big, but they still like to play. They use everything as toys — a branch lying on the ground, a leaf, or even a blade of grass.

The youngest elephants like to climb on top of each other. When big brother is sleeping, the little ones think it is the perfect time to jump on him.

The adults like to play, too, especially during the rainy season when it is easy to find plenty of food.

Two young males wrestle with each other. Face to face, with trunks laced together, they push back and forth. They butt heads to see who is the strongest.

The leader of the herd watches these games. She knows that the males will leave when they are fully grown. She has taught the other females how to find the water holes and how to lead the herd down the same paths that the herd has traveled for many generations. After her, another female of the herd will take over.

The females of the herd stay together and take care of each other.

Goodbye, little male

The leader of the herd is nearly 60 years old. She has had a baby almost every five years, and her youngest son is now 12 years old. It is time for him to leave the herd. He will join a group of male teenage elephants. His female cousin, who was born the same year, will stay with the herd. When she is 14 years old, she will be old enough to have her first baby.

At nightfall, the herd heads towards the woods. They meet another family of elephants. It seems that they are happy to see them. The animals run toward each other. They wrap their trunks together; they clap their ears, and continue together towards the woods.

At the end of the rainy season, each family goes its own way.

Once there were millions

Curiously enough, elephants have always been attracted by humans, their only real enemy. Humans have always been fascinated by elephants, whose memory and intelligence are surprising. However, an elephant's ivory tusks are so valuable that people have killed many elephants to get them. Hunting and the destruction of the environment have brought the elephants close to extinction. Laws forbidding the sale of ivory are our best hope for saving these gentle giants.

In 1989, the government of Kenya burned hundreds of tusks that had been confiscated from hunters.

The human enemy

In 1970, there were two million elephants in Africa. Since then, the demand for ivory has gone up so much that its price per pound has gone from $2.00 to over $200. This is a fortune compared to the average salary of most Africans. Today, less than one quarter of the elephants are left. The great males were the first to be hunted because they have the biggest tusks. Now, even the females and the young with tiny tusks are hunted. At this rate, the elephant could soon become extinct.

People on the trail of the elephants.

The white pits of the ivory palm are covered with brown skin that has to be pulled off before the pit can be carved.

What scientists are doing

Many scientists are studying elephants to learn more about their behavior. The scientists can recognize each elephant by its ears: their shape, nicks along the edges, and the veins. Some scientists have recorded the very low sounds of elephants talking when they are miles away from each other.

What we can do

Saving the elephant has been a top priority since 1989 when most countries signed an agreement that forbids the sale of ivory. Some countries refused to sign the agreement, so we must all do our part and refuse to buy anything made of ivory. The rate of hunting has gone down and scientists say that the elephant can be saved.

No migration allowed

To protect the elephants, reserves have been created, but elephants on reserves cannot migrate to new areas to find food. When the population of elephants grows, they need more space. This space is no longer available because the population of humans has grown, too, and they have cut down the forests and planted crops on the land.

What is coroso?

There is a substitute for ivory called coroso. This is the pit of a fruit that grows on a palm tree. The pit has the color and texture of ivory and even polishes easily.

The elephant family

The elephant is unique. It is a member of the Proboscidean family, which means "animal with a trunk." The woolly mammoths that lived during the Ice Age also belonged to this family. The mammoths disappeared about 9,000 years ago. Now the family has only two members. One lives on the continent of Africa; the other lives on the continent of Asia.

▲

The hyrax is the elephant's closest living relative. This little animal, no bigger than a rabbit, hardly resembles an elephant!

The elephants of Africa that live in the forests tend to be smaller than those that live on the plains. They have thin, straight tusks, and relatively small, round ears.

▶

26

▲

The Asian elephant has much smaller ears than the African elephant. Its forehead is curved and has a bump on top. Its trunk has only one sensitive lip. The females do not have any tusks, and many males do not, either. With no tusks, they are safe from the ivory hunters!

The elephant of the African savanna ▶ is the biggest of all land animals. The male weighs nearly 8 tons and is about 11 feet tall. These elephants have enormous ears, and huge tusks that curve outward. The tusks of an old male can weigh as much as 200 pounds each.

Photograph credits:
All photographs by Christine and Michel Denis-Huot except the following:
A. BEIGNET: p 24 (bottom).
GAMMA: Willets/Camérapix p 24 (top).
BIOS: J. Mallwitz p 25 (bottom); R. Seitre p 27 (top).

We would like to thank Pierre Pfeffer of the laboratory of mammals at the French National Museum of Natural History for his scientific counsel.